THE KINGDOM & THE DRAGON

A BUSINESS FABLE

JONATHAN DAVID LEWIS

MPATH PUBLISHING

The Kingdom and The Dragon: A Business Fable
Copyright © 2024 by Jonathan David Lewis. All Rights Reserved.
No part of this publication may be reproduced, stored in a retrieval system or transmitted, in any form or by any means—electronic, mechanical, photocopying, recording, or otherwise—without prior written permission from the publisher, except for the inclusion of brief quotations in a review.

For more information about this title or to order other books and/or electronic media, contact the publisher: (888) 821-2999

Printed in the United States of America

For Steve, the dragon slayer.

Regnum et Draco

∽∝∽

You can't feel it till it pulls you.

You can't hold it in your lair.

You can't see it till they show you.

You can't know it till you're there.

∽∝∽

Once upon a time

Business is like a young hero who sets out to slay a dragon.

The dragon haunts the village. Supplies are delayed. Merchants charge exorbitant sums. The people suffer. The local governor is so afraid that he just stays in his pitiful castle all day and writes press releases. But the town crier has never been better. The worse things get, the more people click on his panicked posts.

The governor smiles to himself as he hits send on another press release, *Governor Signs Order to Stop Dragon for Good*. Curiously, the town crier uses the headline word for word in his post.

The merchants sell anti-dragon products in the village square, yelling at passersby, "Two coins for the Warrior's Will dragon repellent! Buy one get the Slay Spray half off! Never worry about the dragon again!"

A young farm girl named Amalia loves to visit the village. But the dragon menace ruins everything. People talk about the danger, but nobody does anything about it. The governor promises to protect the village, but the village isn't safe. The merchants boast about their bravery, but they never act brave.

One evening, while Amalia is feeding her family's livestock and her parents are preparing dinner in their farmhouse, she feels a hot rush of wind at her back.

She closes her eyes tightly. She doesn't want to believe it, but the smell confirms her fears.

The dragon is on the hunt for gold.

Amalia spins around and freezes. She watches as the dragon bears down on her parents' home like an eagle on a mouse.

In a flash, the roof is gone, and fire fills the house.

She stares in agony.

Just as quickly as it arrived, the dragon flaps its wings, shoots into the air, and flies away. Amalia runs toward the fire and dares to hope.

She sees her father as he limps out the door, her mother in his arms.

Mother is gone.

The fire from the smoldering home flickers in Amalia's eyes. She runs into the house, finds her phone, and swears to never return until the dragon is dead.

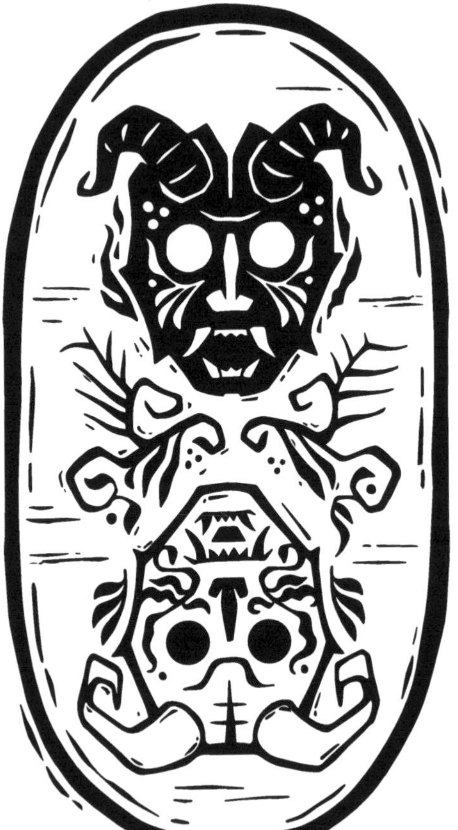

THE YOUNG WILL SLAY THE DRAGONS

Business is like Amalia locked in ferocious battle with the dragon.

"Hey, dragon!" Amalia quavers.

"I know why you're here!" the dragon seethes.

Amalia darts behind a boulder just as the dragon's fire blackens the rock.

"I'm here to stop you!" Amalia screams through the thick smoke, clenching her sword and clinging to the boulder.

The dragon hovers just above the ground and roars, "Liar!"

The villagers gather in large numbers, encircling the area while looking for the best view. Smoke and fire fill the air as merchants sell roasted nuts to the famished onlookers. The town crier breathlessly documents the action. Clicks are through the roof. But the governor doesn't dare leave his castle. He only peeks through the windows, writing and rewriting the next day's press release in his head.

"I'll rid this land of dragons for good!" Amalia says through gritted teeth, her bare feet cut and burned by the rock and flame.

"I see you, liar," the dragon menaces.

Through the flames, Amalia barely makes out the soft belly of the beast.

A weak spot, she thinks, as her heart swells inside her.

Amalia bolts out from behind the boulder, lifts her sword, and thrusts it into the heart of the creature.

The dragon shouts, "AAARRRRRGGGGGH," and falls to the earth like a comet. The crowd swoons in shock.

The mountain of scales lies as still as stone. Amalia cautiously hobbles toward the beast, her singed clothes still smoking. The light from the crowd's phones surrounds Amalia like fireflies at dusk.

She stares into the face of the corpse. Her heart pulses inside her. Something about the dragon makes her sad.

Just then the dragon's eyes blink open. The crowd shudders.

"How could you do this to me?" the dragon shrills. "Don't you know who I am? Don't you know what I've done for this place?!" Mustering all its strength, the dragon stands, screaming, "I...AM...THE—"

Amalia's sword cuts through the dragon's throat like a river through a gorge. The crowd erupts in cheers. The foul creature is dead at last.

Amalia drops her sword and falls to her knees. She takes a selfie and sends a message to her dad that reads, *I did it! (fire emoji)*.

"I did it," she says out loud with a twinge of surprise. Then, louder with a laugh, she says, "I did it!"

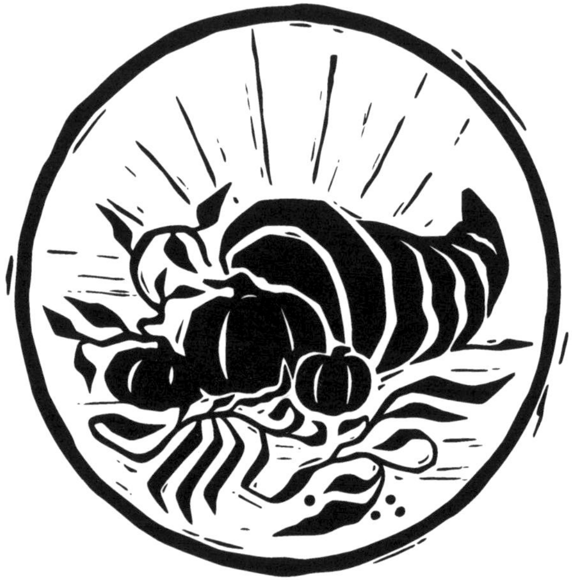

The victors get the gold

Business is like a barefoot Amalia standing triumphantly atop the dragon.

She puts down her phone and tries to pick up all the gold.

She can't believe it. There is so much treasure. Far too much to carry out of the dragon's lair with her own two hands.

So she takes just one coin and swears to come back later.

She goes to the village. The people shout in jubilation.

"Thank you, Amalia!" they cry through the streets. "Take these vegetables as a gift. Take these chickens as well. You can even have our sheep and cattle. We're free!"

Without the dragon, the people have nothing to fear. The town crier's clicks drop seventy percent. The merchants leave as quickly as they arrived, their intentions as exposed as their empty solutions.

The governor is dragged out of the castle and mocked in the town square. He cowers before the bright sun, trying to hide his delicate pale skin from the light. Gold coins spill from his packed pockets. An impoverished crowd watches him scramble to pick up the coins from the ground, his mouth and fingernails stained with gold dust.

The villagers lift Amalia onto their shoulders and shout, "Amalia is our queen! All hail Amalia!"

"Our queen cannot be barefoot!" they exclaim. "We will use scales from the dead dragon to fashion armored shoes. A gift for our queen! The Dragon Slayer!"

Over the next few weeks, Amalia takes more selfies with the villagers than ever before. And with all the gifts, she has more stuff than she could ever imagine.

But she can't forget the gold.

While preparing to take over the governor's castle, she sends guards to the dragon's lair to keep the treasure safe.

She holds that beautiful single gold coin in her hand and smiles. *I did it!* she thinks.

News of the dragon's demise spreads quickly. People from the countryside pour into the village. There is abundance again. The village grows and grows until it isn't a village anymore.

It's a kingdom.

Events unfold at a dizzying pace. Amalia can barely hang on. The kingdom is growing like crazy.

When bridges must be built, roads engineered, or city squares constructed, Amalia isn't concerned about the kingdom's treasury. She just sends for more gold from the dragon's lair.

And when the people are exhausted from all the growth, she reminds them of the monstrous dragon and how important it is to never let something like that happen again.

"This kingdom will always be strong. These leaders will always be brave. And these people will never be hurt again," she says with absolute conviction.

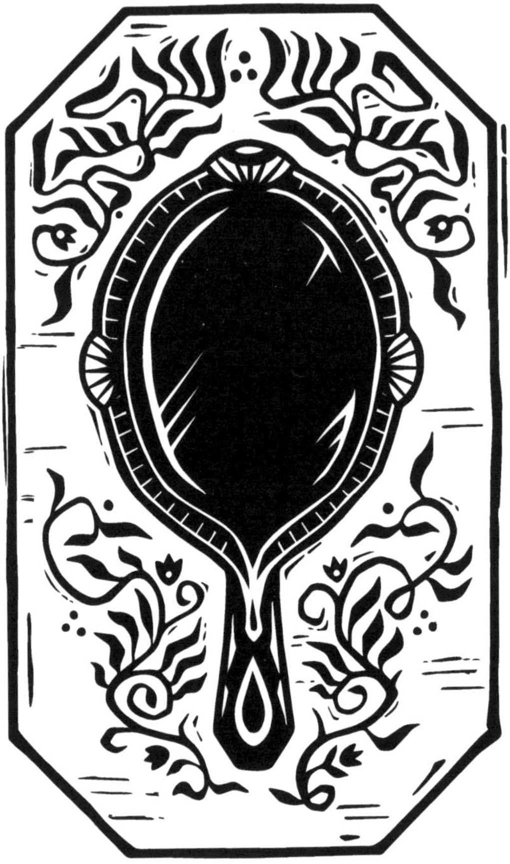

The kings expand their kingdoms

Business is like Queen Amalia sitting on her throne, sending emails and making edicts.

The kingdom is bursting at the seams. Amalia spends her days managing her realm, negotiating treaties, and sending her armies to war.

The kingdom is so successful that she doesn't worry about the dragon's treasure much these days. Her wealth is so great that she even fashions her throne out of some of the dragon's gold.

New throne for my (castle emoji)! #Blessed, her post reads.

Most importantly, she keeps that single gold coin in a locket near her heart to remind her of that evil dragon that she slayed.

Now that Amalia doesn't have to worry about the dragon anymore, she can focus on other issues, like expanding her kingdom.

Advisors fill her halls. Foreign emissaries request her attention. And she just loves working with the court architects to design her big, new, "forever" castle.

"Did you see my late thirteenth-century modern-rustic mood board?" she proudly asks an architect while flipping through her phone.

Sometimes Amalia thinks running the kingdom isn't as fun as it used to be. Sure, she loves her subjects and would do anything for them. But leading the realm just isn't as thrilling as establishing it. Every so often, she daydreams about running away to slay another dragon.

Yet serious matters demand her attention. Her people need her wisdom, and her golden throne is far too beautiful to simply walk away from.

News arrives that another war has broken out along her expanding borders. Plans must be made. Armies must be mustered. And lands must be conquered.

"Armorer!" Amalia calls. "It is time for war. Forge for me the strongest suit of armor in the kingdom."

Admiring the dragon scales on her armored shoes, Amalia continues, "And make sure my new suit of armor matches my people's gift. When their queen stands before her army, they shall know that the Dragon Slayer leads them into battle!"

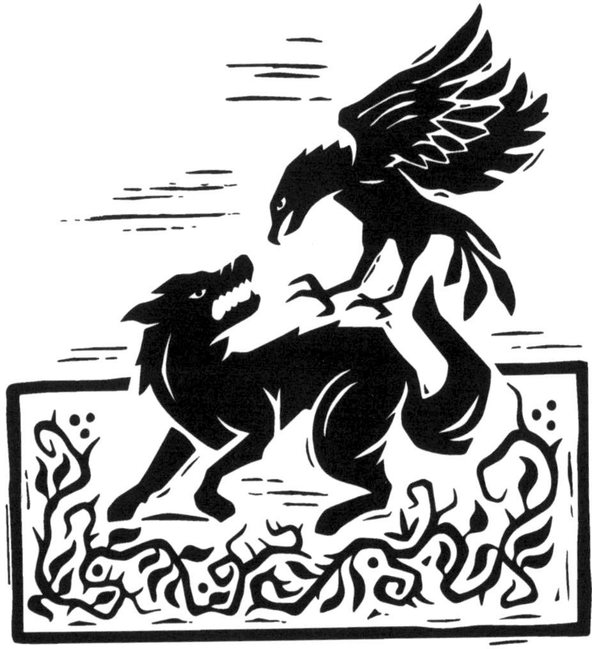

The people ask for moats

Business is like Amalia in her big, new, "forever" castle reading yet another urgent message from the borderlands.

(Crown emoji)! Villages are (fire emoji). Barbarians. 911. Send help, the message reads.

The constant barrage of problems wears Amalia down. She interrupts her budget meeting to read the message out loud.

"What should we do?" she asks in a weakening voice.

Her advisors can't agree. Her borders used to spread far and wide. But now the barbarians attack more frequently, and the kingdom is shrinking. Her subjects are so far from the capital they're difficult to protect. Plus, all of this distracts from her vacation plans.

"I told you we should have waited to attack Competistan until the spring," a smug advisor pipes up while leaning back in his gold-plated chair.

"We didn't have a choice!" another replies with one eye on the bulging grapes in the middle of the table.

A third hungrily counts a pile of gold coins on the table and suggests, "The people are vulnerable, my queen. We must build up our defenses immediately."

Amalia feels like the whole kingdom is on her shoulders. *This used to be fun,* she thinks. *I'm not sure I'm the right person for this anymore.*

Another message arrives in the middle of the commotion. *The merchants' guild is (angry face emoji). They're demanding patrols to protect the roads.*

Amalia's patience is wearing thin. She raises her hand to quiet the room and lets her eyes linger toward the windows.

"We have come so far and built so much," Amalia reminisces, wearily gazing upon her realm. Her kingdom is so large that she can't see where her family's farm is anymore. She can't even remember where it stood.

All eyes are on Amalia as she speaks. "Our people suffer and cry for help. We must protect the people. Prepare to build the greatest defenses in the world."

Some advisors smile. Others roll their eyes and cross their arms. One obliviously nibbles on the edge of a gold coin. But no one dares to speak openly against the queen's orders.

"Who is more precious than our queen?" an advisor asks between chomps of an apple. "Let us also fashion the biggest shield in the land to protect her from our enemy's arrows!"

The queen's court explodes with activity as emails go out to the kingdom to build up the village walls, dig deep castle moats, and forge the queen's shield.

Amalia hates to do it, but she knows she has to raise taxes to pay for the extensive defenses. Now that her borders are shrinking, she can't take gold from all the other kingdoms anymore.

Most of all, she is bothered by reports of unrest among her subjects.

Don't they know how much I care? she muses as she gazes into the distance. *Maybe I care too much.*

Amalia tries to stretch in her suit of armor, but she can barely move with all the weight. Her back hurts, her feet are sore, and her stomach pangs with hunger.

Amalia picks up her phone to order dinner. *I've given them so much. Why can't they just appreciate what I've done?* she thinks with a sigh.

After a day like that, all she wants to do is disappear into her castle, put on her favorite show, and fall asleep.

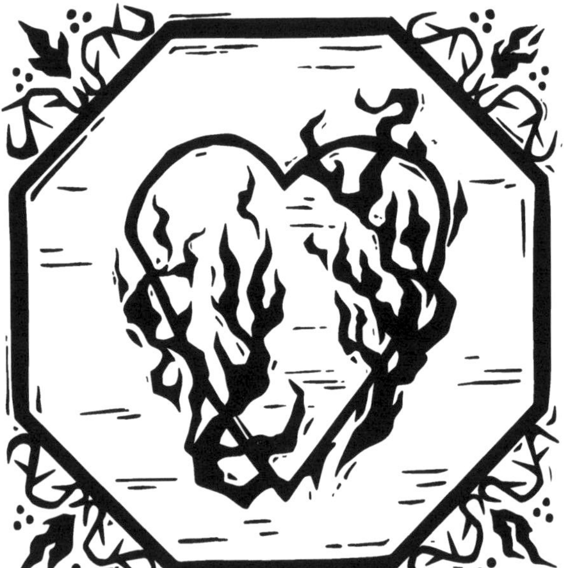

The fire fills the throat

Business is like Amalia sinking into her golden throne, numb to the chaos around her.

She just left her seventh meeting of the day. Her calendar shows ten more await her.

All she gets is bad news these days.

Where are my allies when I need them? she broods. *Where are the mercenaries that I pay so handsomely? Why aren't my governors doing more?*

"I can't do everything for everyone," she mumbles, absent-mindedly touching the locket where she keeps her dragon coin.

Most of today's meetings are about rumors of a rebellion. The kingdom is under siege, and all the warring increases taxes. The people are hungry and complaining.

Amalia tries to gather herself. The next meeting is at hand. The room is packed with advisors. The nervous energy is palpable.

An advisor with shifty eyes opens the meeting. "My queen, a decision must be made. The people have gathered outside to make trouble. We could have rioting even this night."

Another rubs a coin between two fingers and suggests, "If the people murmur, let us mint more coin and declare a tax holiday."

"Tax holiday?" another advisor bursts mid-drink. "Our collections are down! We need a tax increase to simply fund the kingdom!"

"Whatever we do," yet another speaks up, "we must act fast. Our spies report Competistan is preparing an invasion. Our defenses will not hold."

Feeling something swelling in her chest, Amalia demands, "Armorer! Bring me a helmet. I can't think with all this noise."

The armorer approaches Amalia with a helmet forged to match her shield, her suit, and her shoes. The metal is thick and the artistry masterful. It's the most beautiful thing Amalia's ever seen.

Armor fit for the Dragon Slayer, she thinks.

The armorer slowly places the helmet upon Amalia's head. It hides everything but her dull eyes. The outside world goes silent.

Suddenly, the doors to the throne room slam open. The captain of the castle guard staggers in with urgent news.

"Competistan has surrounded the castle!" he cries, one arm on the door and the other grasping his chest plate. "And the townspeople are attacking their own gates!"

The room explodes with advice and demands. Some yell at the guard. Some run to the windows. Others quietly slip toward the side doors.

"ENOUGH!" Amalia bellows. "Must I do everything around here?"

But no one can hear her through the armor.

Stunned by the lack of response, Amalia reaches for the dragon gold in her locket and shrills, "I...AM...THE...QUEEN!"

Still, no one notices.

Furious, she takes the dragon gold, places it in her mouth, and swallows.

The frantic room stops in horror. Amalia's eyes widen in surprise. Even she is shocked by her urge to eat the gold.

The light of a thousand torches floods the throne room through the windows. It is silent but for the raucous throng outside. Shouts are heard as the guards brace the castle gates.

Finally, a shuddering advisor with bulging eyes and a bead of sweat on his forehead takes a gold coin from the table and places it in his mouth.

Another advisor nervously eyes his peers, removes a ring from his finger, and slowly nibbles on it.

Suddenly, three people leap upon the table and gnaw on a golden lampstand. The room thrashes as people gorge themselves on gold jewelry, gold curtains, gold clothes, and gold ornaments.

Wild-eyed advisors claw, cut, choke, and rip. Gold is everywhere, dripping down hands and mouths like burst grapes. Someone stands back recording with their phone and cackling. Another person screams as someone sits on their shoulders gobbling a golden tiara.

Watching her court devour the room, Amalia's dead eyes fill with fire. The dragon scales on her armored shoes quiver and bulge. The scales spread up her legs like a hungry virus, growing across her breastplate, over her shield, and throughout her helmet.

Amalia rises from her throne like an erupting volcano.

"YOU THIEVES!" she booms. "YOU ARE STEALING MY GOLD!" A tail and wings burst out of her armor like cannons. "My enemies are thieves! My advisors are thieves! Even my people steal from me!"

Amalia looks down at her hands and instead sees claws. She extends her new wings and stares at her people in disgust. "They steal from without, and they steal from within," she fumes.

THE KINGDOM & THE DRAGON

Like a spark in a powder house, the crowded throne room explodes as Amalia sets her frenzied advisors aflame. Unsatisfied, she blasts out the door and rises above the castle in fury.

"It is time to reclaim what is mine!" Amalia bellows.

Amalia's darting eyes search the countryside from house to house for gold. She stalks her kingdom, now dotted in flames. The people's cries rise to the sky alongside the smoldering remains of her destruction.

"How could they do this to me?" she laments.

A shimmering light in a window of a farmhouse catches her eye. "**MY GOOOOOLD!**" She flies toward the home like an eagle toward its prey.

In a flash, the roof is gone and fire fills the house.

Amalia's eyes search for gold but find only the glow from a phone screen.

"Liars!" she roars. "There is no gold here! Where have you hidden it?!"

Disappointed, Amalia leaves to find more gold. She stops just for a moment and turns around to look at the burning house. Amalia sees what looks like three trembling figures holding each other outside the collapsing home.

"Don't they know who I am?" she rumbles. "Don't they know what I've done for this place?"

Just then Amalia hears a voice yelling behind her. She turns around to see a pitiful youth with a rusty sword and a phone.

"Hey, dragon!" the voice quavers.

∽∞⌒

The young will slay the dragons.

The victors get the gold.

The kings expand their kingdoms.

The people ask for moats.

Then the fire fills the throat.

∽∞⌒

The End

BUSINESS TIME

Our research, conducted among thousands of business executives across hundreds of industries in the United States, has identified five well-documented stages in business. Disruptive organizations set out to slay the dragon and free the people. Accelerating companies rapidly advance to secure their newly won kingdoms. Maturing organizations expand into uncharted territory. Then, as the environment becomes increasingly saturated, once-brave pioneers feel threatened and build walls to defend their domain. As commoditization increasingly overtakes them, they turn to protecting their treasures with sulfur and fire.

These phases of business are cyclical. The risk-taking of Disruption is rewarded by the growth of Acceleration. The adventures of Acceleration lead to the "adulting" of Maturation. The glory of Maturation turns into the challenge of Saturation. The zero-sum arithmetic of Saturation leads to the struggle of Commoditization. Then someone, or something, disrupts the market and a new cycle begins.

As sure as the Earth orbits the sun, businesspeople work to navigate these cycles. And just as nature blooms in the spring and goes dormant in winter, business leaders demonstrate predictable attitudes and behaviors based on the phase with which they're wrestling.

This model helps us understand the cyclical nature of business and how leaders view their identity throughout the cycle. Like all models, it is incomplete, but it provides a framework for understanding where you've been, where you are, and where you might be going.

And most importantly, who you think you are.

DISRUPTION

During Disruption, the task is to slay the dragon, whether it be an unmet consumer need or a corrupt or broken industry. From *The Hobbit's* Smaug to *Sleeping Beauty's* Maleficent, myth and story often depict the dragon as hidden, powerful, and terrifying. This dragon represents chaos and danger, brooding over its dominion with fire and brimstone. It jealously guards the glimmering treasure you seek. This is the call to adventure for the entrepreneurial business leader. Either you slay the dragon, or it slays you.

Companies in Disruption have often seen around a corner. They're breaking new ground and shaking old foundations—sometimes even their own. They've recognized an unmet need, an inefficient process, a broken business model, or an opportunity enabled by new technology. Rather than becoming victims of creative destruction, they're determined to disrupt the market themselves.

Disruption is critical, but it is never enough. The last thing you want to do is disrupt the market solely for someone else. Generating traction and establishing early momentum is urgent. That requires investment capital, the right business model, insight into the evolving (or emerging) market, the right management team, and an endless supply of optimism and perseverance.

Unfortunately, like the skeletons of would-be heroes scattered along the trail to Treasure Mountain, most startups fail to slay the dragon. But for those able to overcome the unknown, treasure awaits.

ACCELERATION

During Acceleration, business is about growing your newly established kingdom. You are done searching for danger, sleeping under the stars, and merely dreaming about the future. You've slain the dragon and earned the spoils. You freed the people, and they love you for it. You now have a kingdom. But ruling over an emerging kingdom is very different from defeating a dragon.

Businesses in Acceleration run on young company adrenaline. They are often small or have spun off from a parent company. The team feels like family, creating a close bond and nurturing culture in what is often a fast-paced environment. Youthful energy, hope, and optimism fuel the company even more than the market success and profitability it aggressively pursues.

Yet this stage presents incredible challenges as well. Accelerating companies struggle with staffing, resources, and achieving scale. To overcome their underdog status, leaders often rally the team around a common enemy, pointing the finger at anti-customer lies or the nefarious behavior of their rivals.

When asked to characterize their biggest Acceleration business challenges, business leaders tend to identify market problems first, including competition, technology, and innovation. Second are internal operational issues such as managing rapid change, team training, and employee retention.

More than anything, accelerating companies are defined by aggressive growth and the challenges and opportunities that come with it. From struggling to keep up with demand and staffing to trying to be all things to all people, they feel acute growing pains. Yet they also have clearly defined objectives, enjoy increasing customer loyalty, and benefit from alignment among the leadership team. All of this adds up to a culture that embraces change and is easily differentiated from competitors.

But you can't stay young forever. Even the hottest new organizations eventually feel the pressure to act like grownups. And when they do, they realize mature businesses play a very different game.

MATURATION

During Maturation, business is about mapping and securing as-yet uncharted territory. It's time to grow up. Similar to the challenges of becoming an adult, growing up in business is hard, unsexy, and as necessary as it is unavoidable. At some point, all children must leave their parents and prove to themselves and the world that they can make it on their own. But the road to becoming an adult requires the sacrifice of immature illusions, mistaken assumptions, and unsustainable freedoms. It's tough to grow up.

Business leaders successfully navigating this phase report that they are achieving their objectives and enjoy a culture that is willing to take creative risks. With competitive differentiation growing, their customers fully understand the company's value and know what it stands for. Maturing companies are getting the hang of things, see their confidence growing, and are enjoying the good life.

Momentum (and the resources it generates) enables them to expand into new markets, which paradoxically represents their greatest challenge. Business is conducted differently at scale, and more opportunity generates more complexity. This dynamic creates new frustrations as they struggle with growth that often outpaces their ability to maintain quality. They also begin to outgrow their internal systems, highlighting the need for more sophisticated talent, tools, and processes. "Adulting" requires discipline, and discipline is no fun.

When asked to characterize their biggest business challenges, leaders in Maturation focus heavily on market concerns, identifying competition as their primary hurdle. Following market concerns are a slew of internal challenges, from the need for a more sophisticated strategy to staffing issues and the necessity of enhanced team training.

Maturing companies also cite regulations as an area of concern. Bureaucrats are always late to the party, but you can count on them to show up. Successful organizations and industries always attract the attention of the regulatory state. In the face of new scrutiny, leaders of maturing companies turn their focus to either self-regulation or influencing regulators.

Growing up is a hard business. Ruling a kingdom isn't for everyone. Most companies struggle with scale and end up staying small. But for those that break through and achieve the scale they seek, success often sows the seeds of decline. That's a problem because Saturation looms right around the corner.

SATURATION

During Saturation, moats and ramparts demand your attention. Your kingdom is large, perhaps extending just beyond your reach. Barbarians are threatening your villages. The people must be protected. The crops must be stored behind castle walls. And your treasure must be guarded behind the drawbridge.

Saturation is when growth stalls, the pie becomes fixed, and the whole mood of the organization changes. Leaders of companies in saturated industries report feeling lost, overthinking things, and becoming more opportunistic than strategic. Stalled growth creates a new sense of tension and urgency in the company as revenue becomes more important than profit and you try to maintain scale.

Saturation reveals the full tragedy of the Law of Diminishing Returns. Organic growth slows, old talents and strategies don't work like they used to, and management begins to flail. This is the time when companies start playing not to lose.

When asked to characterize their biggest business challenges, leaders in Saturation tend to be preoccupied with internal issues, reporting leadership as their top concern. Employee morale and internal communication become troubling. As management's concerns turn inward, the organization becomes self-centered and begins gazing at its own navel.

Saturation is also where price competition rears its ugly head and becomes an area of strategic concern. Consumers have no context by which to question the price of a novel product, but in saturated industries apples-to-apples comparisons are readily made. The forces of commoditization encourage competitors to attempt to steal market share based on price. This new dynamic shifts the customer proposition from value to cost.

Having something to lose is the curse of success—as is the accompanying pride, shame, and denial when growth eventually stalls. Instead of seeking a dragon to slay, the culture starts smelling like sulfur. Instead of focusing your energy on building the kingdom, your thoughts turn to deepening moats and erecting barricades. Playing not to lose creates declining efficacy because Commoditization is inevitably ahead.

COMMODITIZATION

During Commoditization, kingdom politics tend to take priority over kingdom people. Commoditized companies pursue monopolies instead of invention. They seek favor through marriages of state. They hire mercenaries to fight foreign wars. They debase their currency to fund their kingdom's excess. They incur debt to make up for dwindling treasure.

The overwhelming temptation is to pursue rent-seeking, a term describing individuals or organizations that try to increase their own wealth without creating any benefits for others. Having given up on organic growth, business leaders turn their attention away from customers and attempt to change the rules of the game to their benefit rather than pursue innovation and new growth.

This is often done through manipulation of public policy, over-regulation, predatory lawsuits, or the redistribution of resources rather than the pursuit of innovation. You've heard the phrase "follow the money." In this case, just follow the lawyers, lobbyists, and bureaucrats. You'll find the commoditized companies there.

This phase impacts relationships. Stress begins to harm leaders' personal lives as they can't stop worrying about work when they go home. Office gossip becomes a troubling issue, and internal politics get in the way. Leadership's focus increasingly turns to prioritizing revenue over profits as they wage a constant battle with price pressure.

When asked to characterize their biggest business challenges, companies in Commoditization are concerned primarily with a lack of effective internal leadership—sometimes even questioning their own leadership capabilities. Incompetence and miscommunication are also growing concerns. Leaders complain of internal discord and an inability to make decisions; they may even recognize a need for a new business model. They eventually have to admit that the marketplace has changed and they no longer know their place in it.

Feeling lost, leaders in commoditized industries initiate ever-more false starts since they aren't sure what their companies stand for anymore. They lack the vigor to fight new dragons. Their kingdom is large but stuck. Their castle walls and deep moats now feel more like prisons than protection. And their constant battles, increasing debt, debased currency, and over-dependency on others cause their own citizens to question their reign.

Lost, self-centered, and angry, organizations floundering in Commoditization may one day look in the mirror and realize they have become the dragon.

But all is not necessarily lost. Like an apple falling to the ground, where there is death there is the seed of life. And while going through the cycle is inevitable, how you handle each season is not.

Maybe, with each tick of time's incessant progression around the clock, there is another way.

The heart will fix or fold

Business is like Amalia sinking into her golden throne, numb to the chaos around her.

All she gets is bad news these days.

Most of today's meetings are about rumors of a rebellion. The kingdom is under siege. The people are hungry and complaining.

Amalia tries to gather herself. The next meeting is at hand. The room is packed with advisors. The nervous energy is palpable.

Her advisors pipe up with the usual suggestions, but they've tried them all before.

Suddenly, the doors to the throne room slam open. The captain of the castle guard staggers in with urgent news.

"Competistan has surrounded the castle!" he cries, one arm on the door and the other grasping his chest plate. "And the townspeople are attacking their own gates!"

The room explodes with advice and demands. Some yell at the guard. Some run to the windows. Others quietly slip toward the side doors.

Amalia reaches for the dragon coin she keeps in her locket and closes her eyes. Something wants to burst out of her.

All of her adventures fill her mind like a storm at sea. Her mother in her father's arms. The dead dragon at her feet. The kingdom and the gold and the cheering townspeople.

Finally, she takes a deep breath, opens her eyes, and whispers to herself, "Have I forgotten who I am?"

She lifts her head, sits up straight, and takes off her helmet. Her dull eyes sharpen. She beholds her burdened people. Her anxious advisors. Her enemies outside her walls.

Gazing out the window upon her kingdom, Amalia yearns for her old farmhouse.

It feels like something is dying inside of her. But she knows what she must do.

It's time to renew what was never my own, she mourns.

Addressing her treasurer, her eyes flash. "Melt my throne, and tell the people they shall have their tax holiday."

To her generals, she commands, "Go to Competistan, and negotiate terms. Buy me time. I need it."

Amalia stands tall before her throne like a lonely mountain. She looks solemnly into the distance. The room is transfixed. All eyes behold their queen.

Amalia removes the locket from around her neck, pulls out the dragon coin, and holds it in the palm of her hand.

She tries to drop it but knows it's no use. Someone else must wrest it from her hand.

Her heart pulses as she says, "Herald! Send word to the four corners of the kingdom. I seek a youth with fire in their eyes and the will to kill a dragon."

Staring at the coin in her palm, Amalia muses into her golden reflection, *The Dragon Slayer has one more dragon to slay.*

The young will slay the dragons.

The victors get the gold.

The kings expand their kingdoms.

The people ask for moats.

Then the fire fills the throat.

And the heart will fix or fold.

Jonathan David Lewis is the author of *Brand vs. Wild: Building Resilient Brands for Harsh Business Environments* and president of McKee Wallwork, a team of specialists who help companies grow by aligning leadership with employees and companies with customers.

Through his Foundation Series, beginning with *The Kingdom and The Dragon: A Business Fable*, Jonathan seeks to provide timeless wisdom to business leaders operating in an increasingly divisive culture.

When Jonathan isn't writing, speaking, or leading, he is spending time with his wife and three children in their home in enchanting New Mexico.

Made in the USA
Columbia, SC
03 January 2025